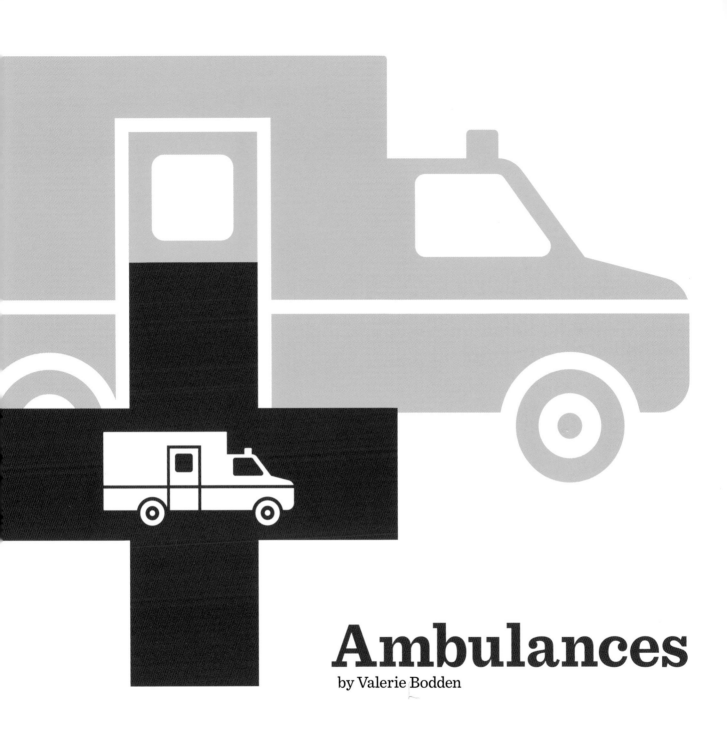

Ambulances

by Valerie Bodden

CREATIVE EDUCATION

RESCUE VEHICLES

Published by **Creative Education**
P.O. Box 227, Mankato, Minnesota 56002
Creative Education is an imprint of The Creative Company
www.thecreativecompany.us

Design and production by **Rob & Damia Design**
Art direction by **Rita Marshall**
Printed by Corporate Graphics in the United States of America

Photographs by **Alamy** (Nancy G Fire Photography/Nancy
Greifenhagen), **Corbis** (Lester Lefkowitz), **Dreamstime** (Nikolais,
Shiyali, Trevoux), **Getty Images** (Pat LaCroix, Richard Leeney,
Andrew Leyerle), **iStockphoto** (Joseph Abbott, Aaron Kohr,
Michael Krinke, Catherine Yeulet, Laura Young)

Library of Congress Cataloging-in-Publication Data

Bodden, Valerie.
Ambulances / by Valerie Bodden.
p. cm. — (Rescue vehicles)
Summary: A fundamental introduction to truck-like rescue vehicles known
as ambulances, including their history, a description of their features, and
how they help people in emergencies.
Includes index.
ISBN 978-1-60818-004-2
1. Ambulances—Juvenile literature.
2. Ambulance service—Juvenile literature. I. Title.

TL235.8.B63 2011
362.18'8—dc22   2009048811
CPSIA: 040110 PO1138

First edition
9 8 7 6 5 4 3 2 1

jj ≤ER⟩
362,188

Contents

Sometimes people need help. They might be hurt. Or they might be lost. When people need **first aid**, an ambulance might come to help them.

Ambulances rush to the site of an emergency

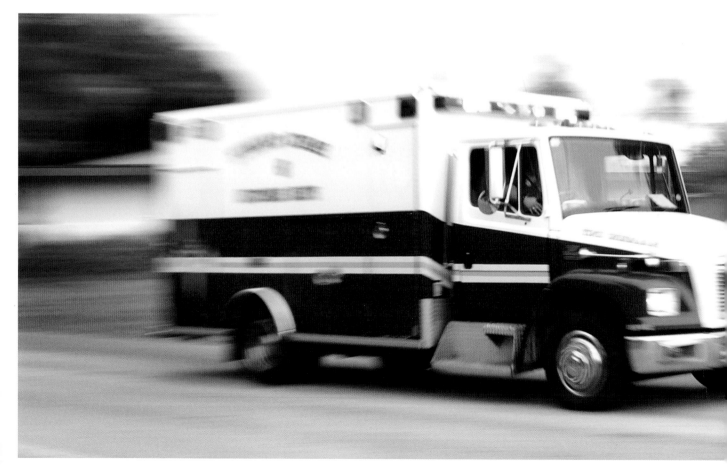

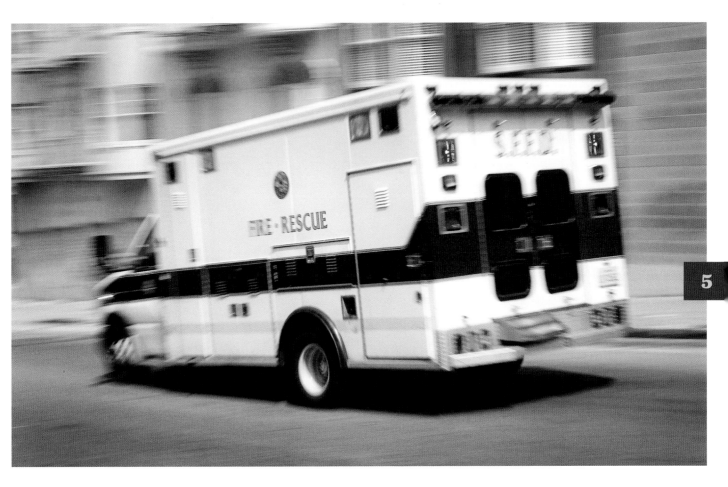

An ambulance is an **emergency** vehicle. It is used to take people who are hurt or sick to the hospital. Ambulances can go very fast.

The first ambulances were used about 200 years ago. They were carts pulled by horses. Later, big cars were used as ambulances.

Many ambulances in the United States are white in color

Today's ambulances look like boxy trucks. Ambulances have flashing lights and loud sirens (*SY-runs*). The lights and sirens warn other drivers to move out of the way.

Ambulances carry first-aid supplies. They have a special bed on wheels called a stretcher. They have bandages, blankets, and medicines. Ambulances have machines to help people breathe, too.

A stretcher can be folded up to fit inside the ambulance

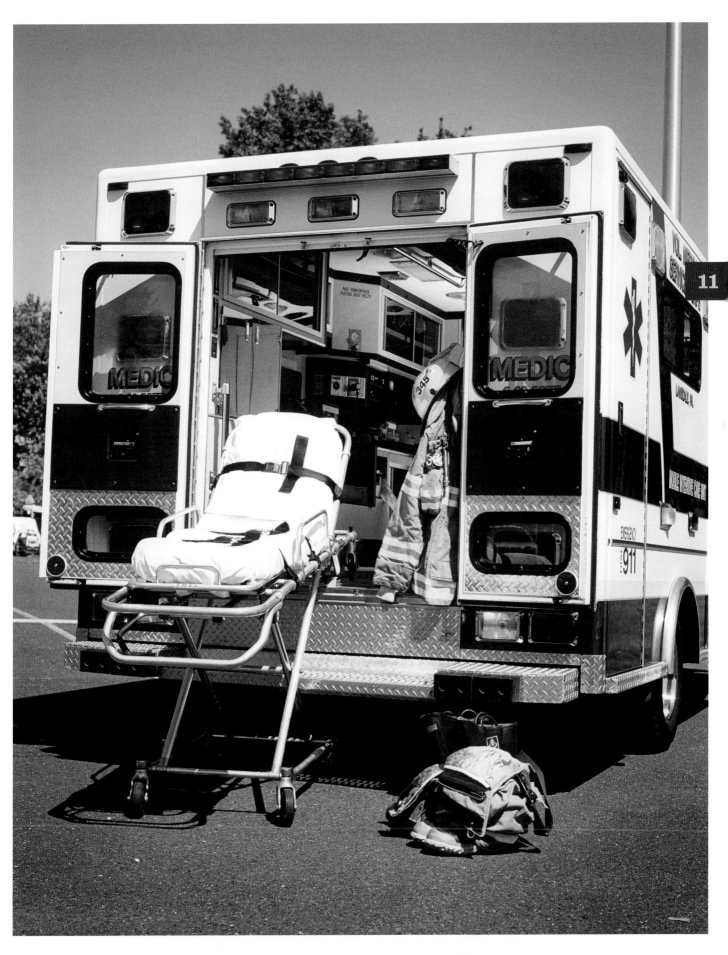

When there is an emergency, a **dispatcher** calls for an ambulance. The ambulance workers jump into action! The workers are called emergency medical technicians (*tek-NISH-uns*), or EMTs. One person drives the ambulance. Another EMT sits next to the driver. If there are more EMTs, they sit in the back.

EMTs (left) respond when they get a call from the dispatcher (above)

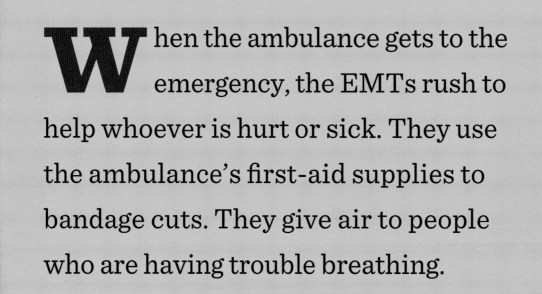

When the ambulance gets to the emergency, the EMTs rush to help whoever is hurt or sick. They use the ambulance's first-aid supplies to bandage cuts. They give air to people who are having trouble breathing.

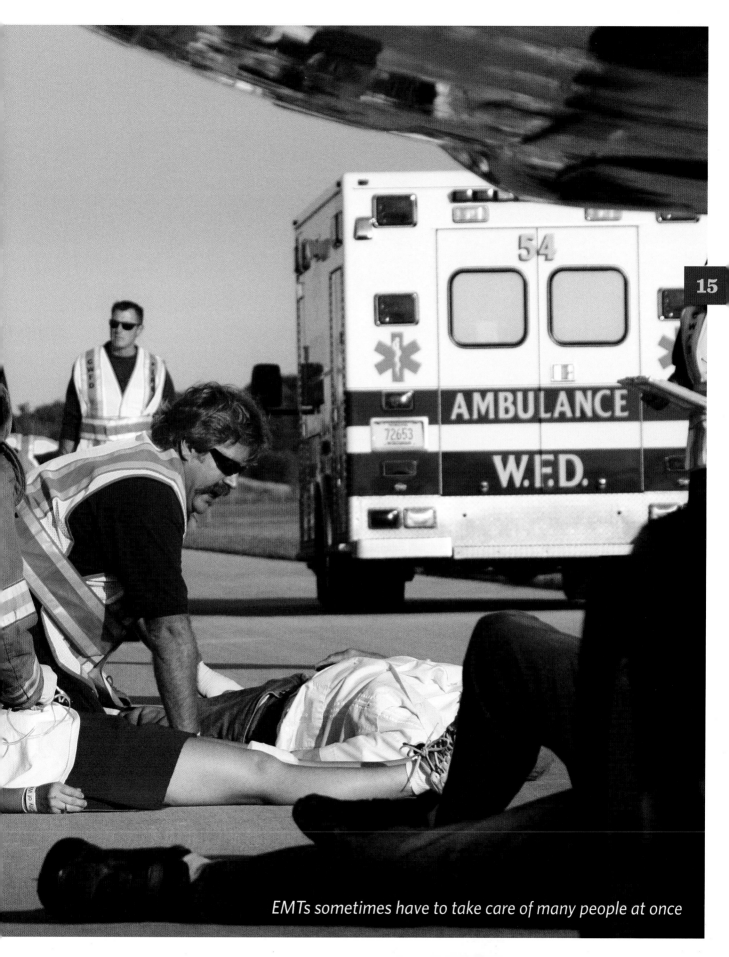

EMTs sometimes have to take care of many people at once

The EMTs put a **patient** who is not able to walk on a stretcher. They wheel it into the back of the ambulance. Then the ambulance speeds to the hospital. The EMTs take care of the patient on the way to the hospital.

Ambulances' back doors can open wide, making it easy to load stretchers

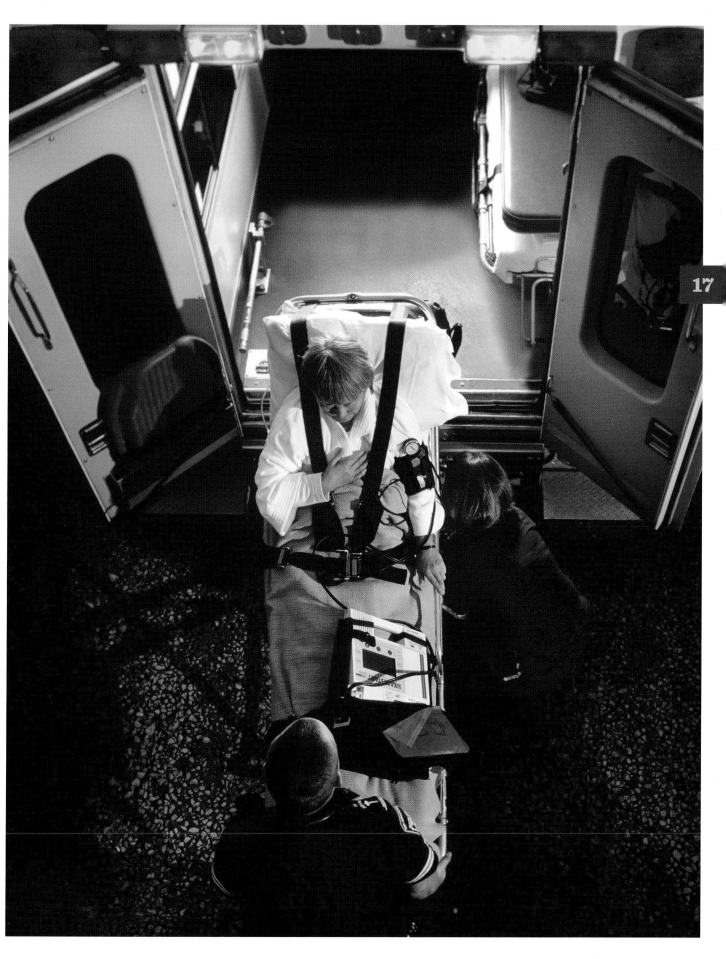

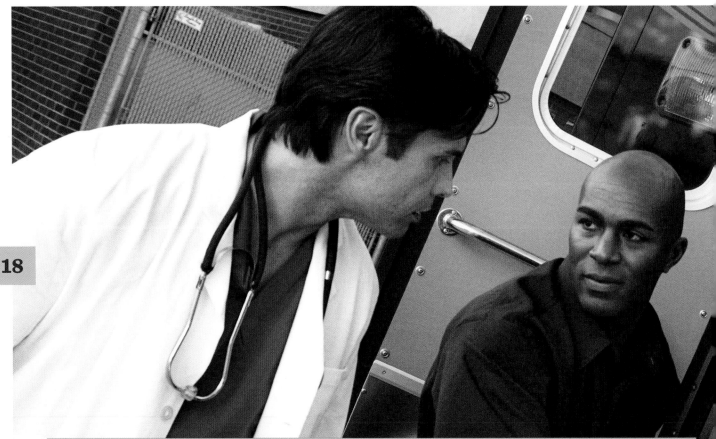

When the ambulance gets to the hospital, doctors and nurses care for the patient. The EMTs drive the ambulance back to its **base**. The base might be at the hospital or at a fire or police station. The EMTs clean the ambulance and check its supplies. They make sure it is ready for the next emergency!

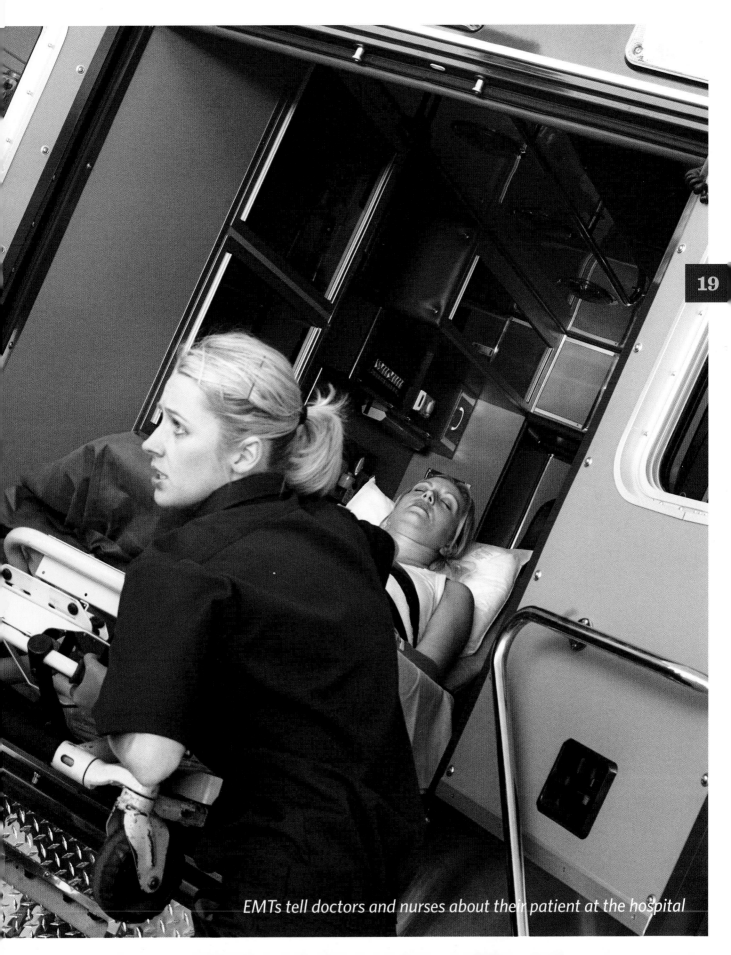

EMTs tell doctors and nurses about their patient at the hospital

Ambulances changed a lot between the 1860s (above) and early 1900s (right)

Early Ambulances

The first horse-drawn ambulances were used in the 1800s. Carts or wagons followed armies of soldiers during wars. They carried soldiers who were hurt to hospitals. In the 1900s, new vehicles called cars were used as ambulances. After a while, these ambulances were used to carry other hurt or sick people in cities and towns, too.

Glossary

base

the place where an emergency vehicle is kept when it is not being used

dispatcher

a person whose job is to get phone calls about emergencies and then send out rescue vehicles

emergency

something bad that happens suddenly, such as a car accident or fire

first aid

help given to someone who is sick or hurt before the person gets to a hospital

patient

a person who needs medical help

Read More

Gordon, Sharon. *What's Inside an Ambulance?* New York: Marshall Cavendish, 2004.

Manolis, Kay. *Ambulances.* Minneapolis: Bellwether Media, 2008.

Web Sites

Colac Ambulance Station's Kid's Page
http://www.colacambulance.com/colac_kids.htm

Have fun with ambulance activities.

What's Inside an Ambulance?
http://www.roanoke.com/
multimedia/360s/rescue.html

Take a tour of the inside of an ambulance.

Index